CROSS STITCH
FLOWERS

Sophie H

Photographs: Régis Baudonnet
Text: Isabelle Contreau

SEARCH PRESS

Cross Stitch
Flowers
introduction

Cross stitch is one of the easiest stitches and can be embroidered on any fabric with any type of thread. All you need to know is how to count and how to follow cross stitch patterns!

Created by young, contemporary designers, the 400 brightly coloured designs in this book are innovative and simple to make. Each double page spread suggests a subject, variations and one or two borders. Four composite scenes and two alphabets complete the collection.

This book, packed full of ideas, is the ideal starting point for designing and making your own cross stitch creations.

Both novice and experienced stitchers can use this book as a source of ideas: flick through, dip in, mix them up, change the colours, use different fabrics and compose new designs for decorating clothes, bags, tablecloths, napkins – in fact, any item that is made of fabric can be enhanced by the addition of a simple embroidered design.

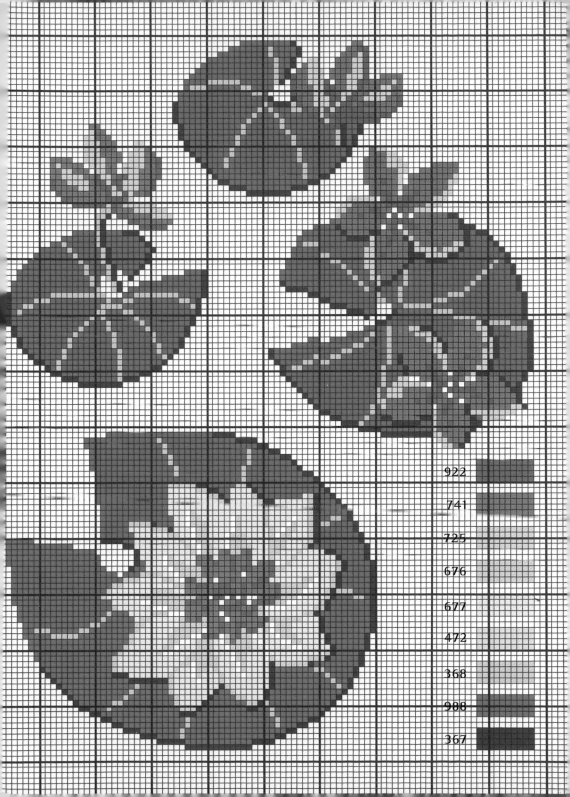

922

741

725

676

677

472

368

988

367

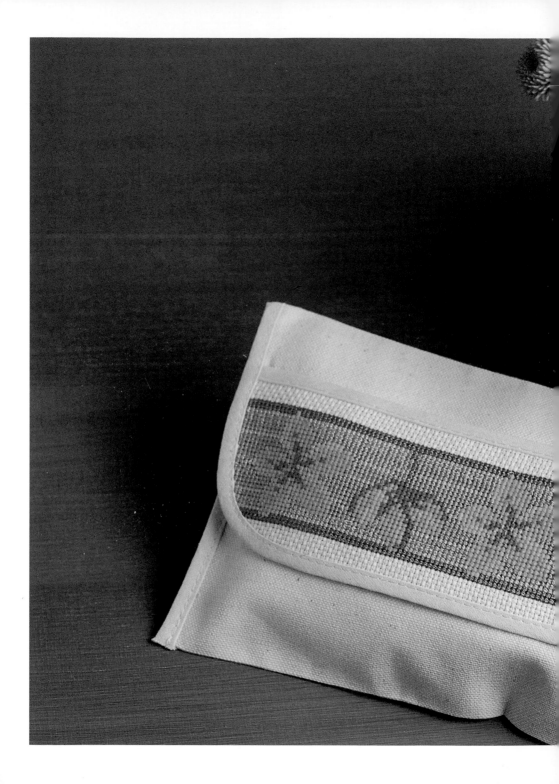

902

816

321

350

720

741

725

3819

906

904

895

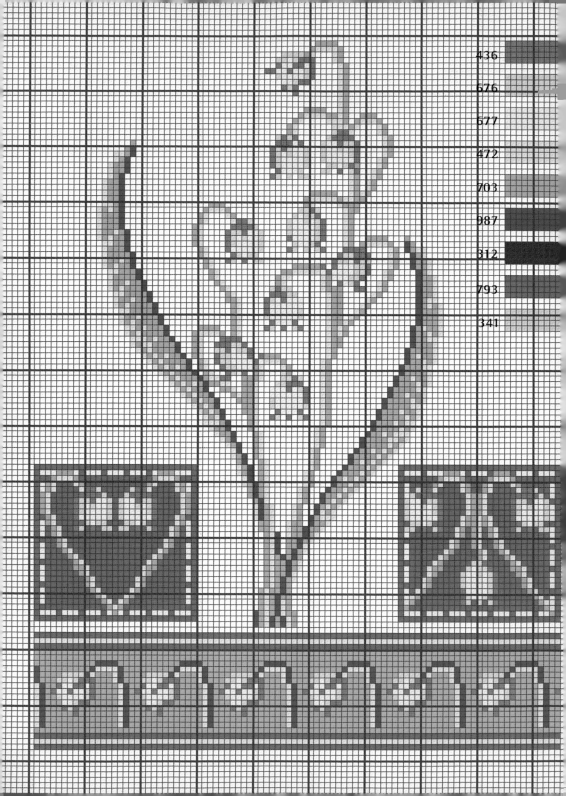

436
676
577
472
703
987
312
793
341

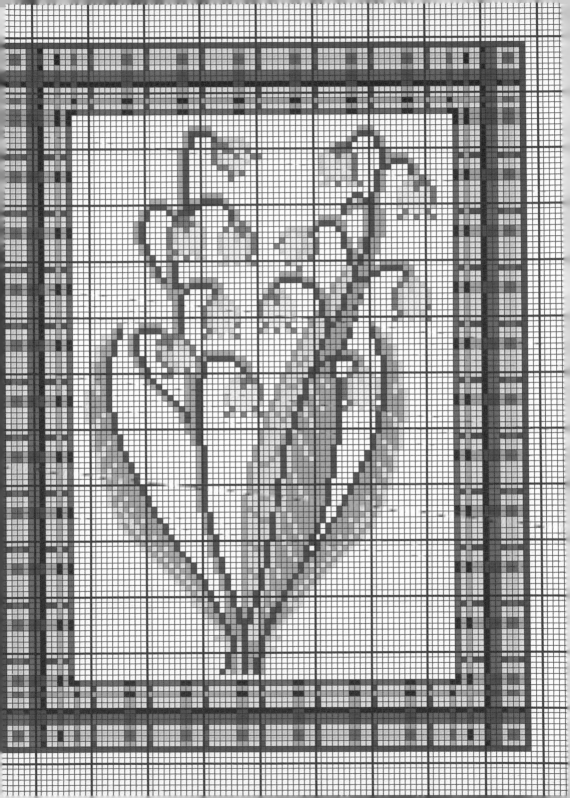

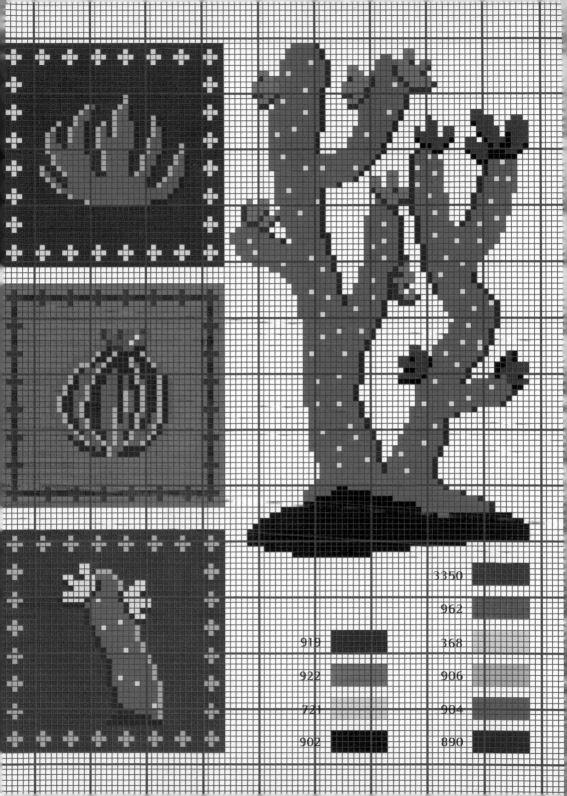

3350

962

919 368

922 906

721 904

902 890

725

988

986

550

553

3689

962

350

600

816

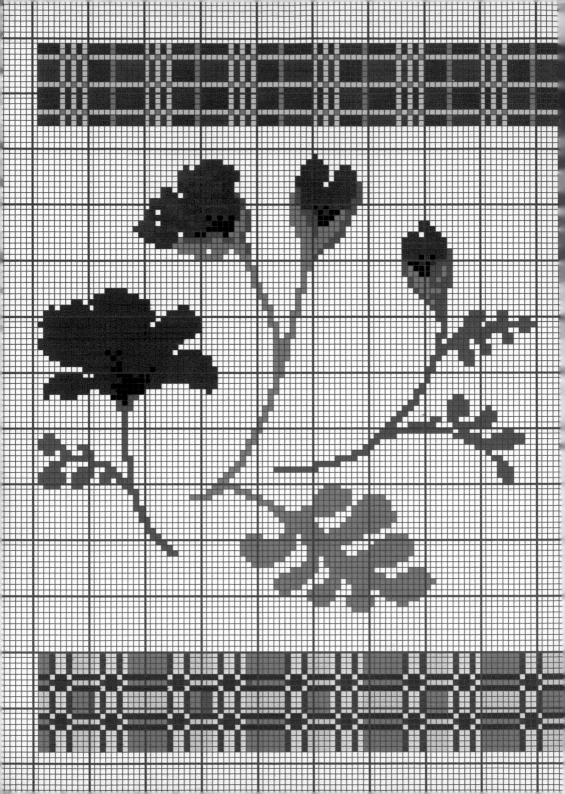

3348

368

988

367

310

613

725

3830

350

600

321

906
987
895
3816
3776
725
721
321
919
3689
3731

613
472
3760
986
988
444
922
321

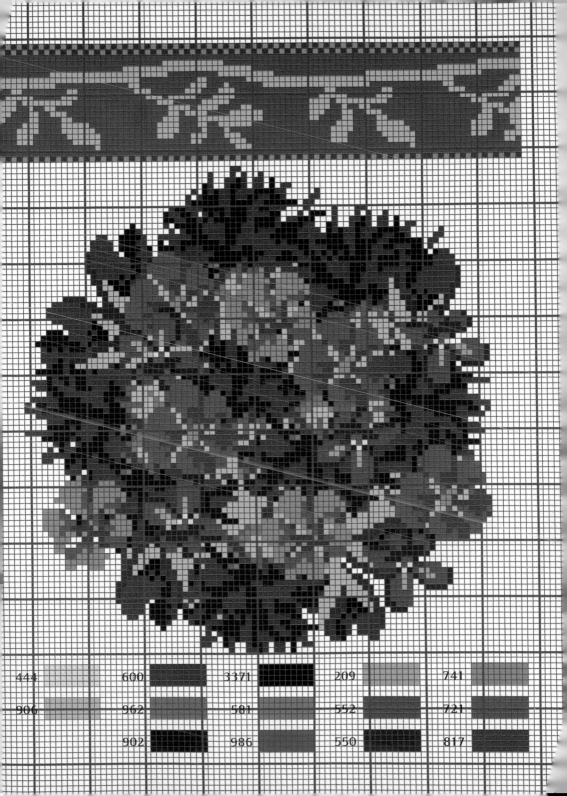

444   600   3371   209   741

906   962   581   552   721

902   986   550   817

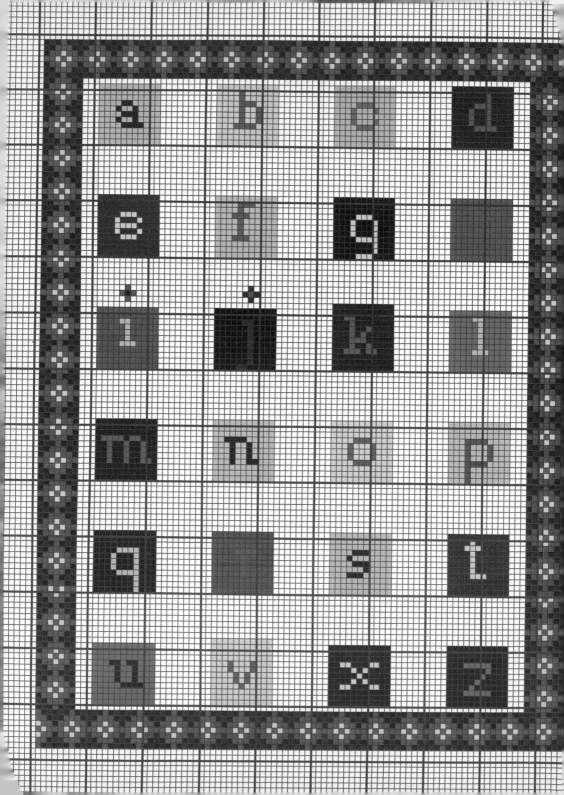

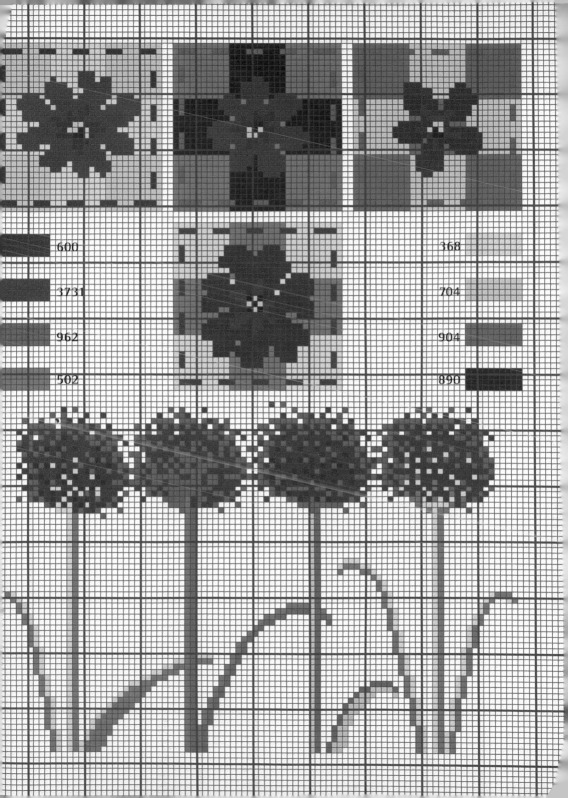

600

3731

962

502

368

704

904

890

725   676   3348

436   677   703

919   368   987

368

987

895

502

676

444

721

321

902

3689

3731

3821 3816 341

676 312 3761

988 518 3830

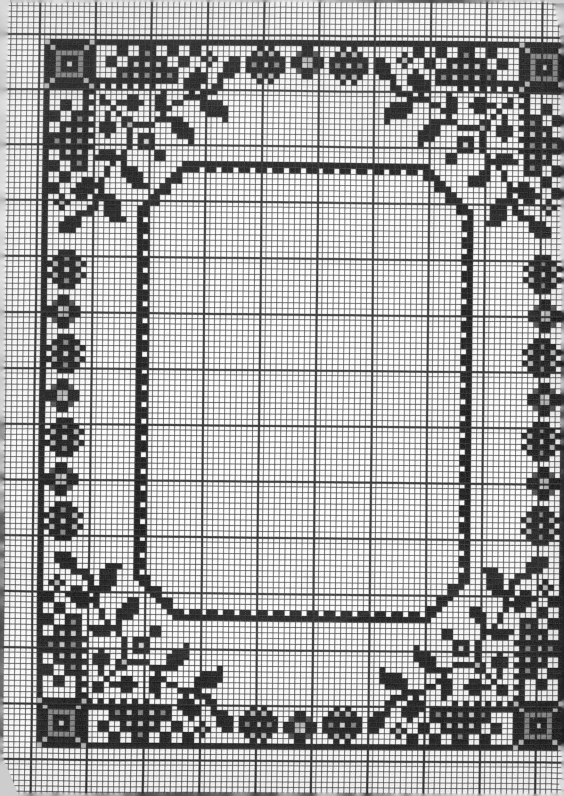

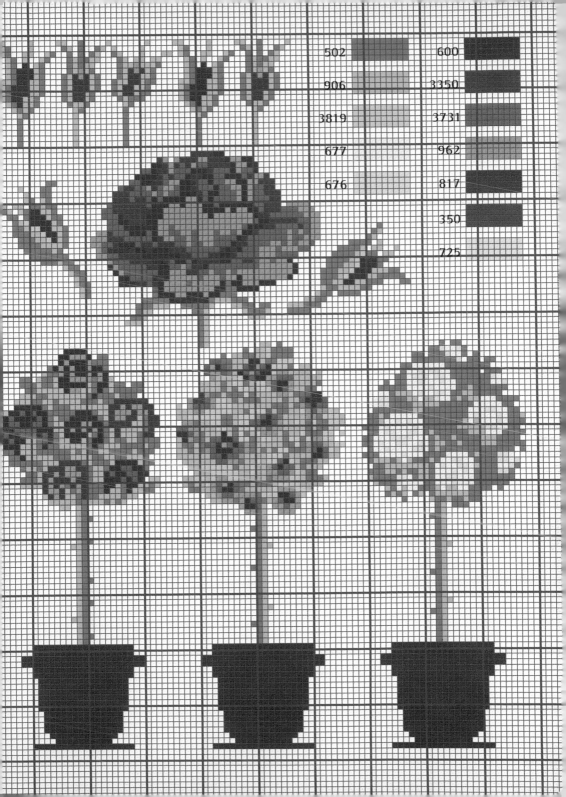

502   600

906   3350

3819   3731

677   962

676   817

350

725

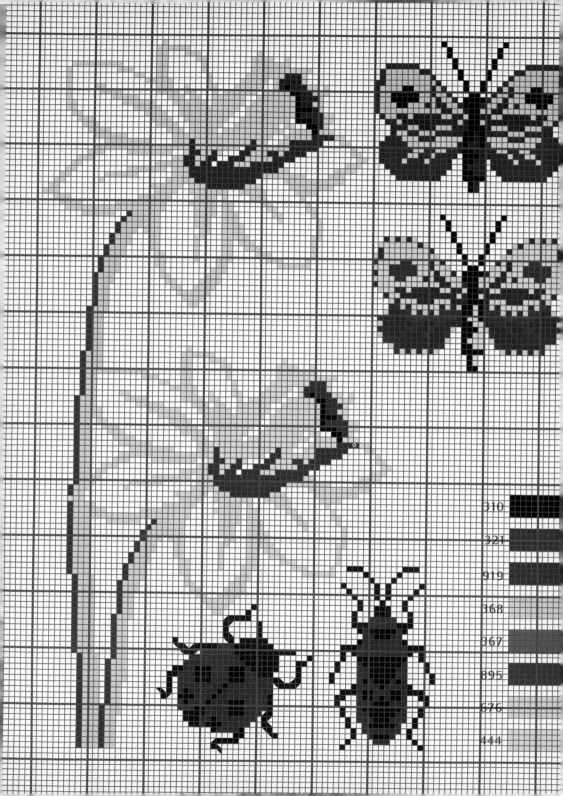

310

321

919

368

367

895

976

444

550
552
208
368
988
987
895
721
741
725

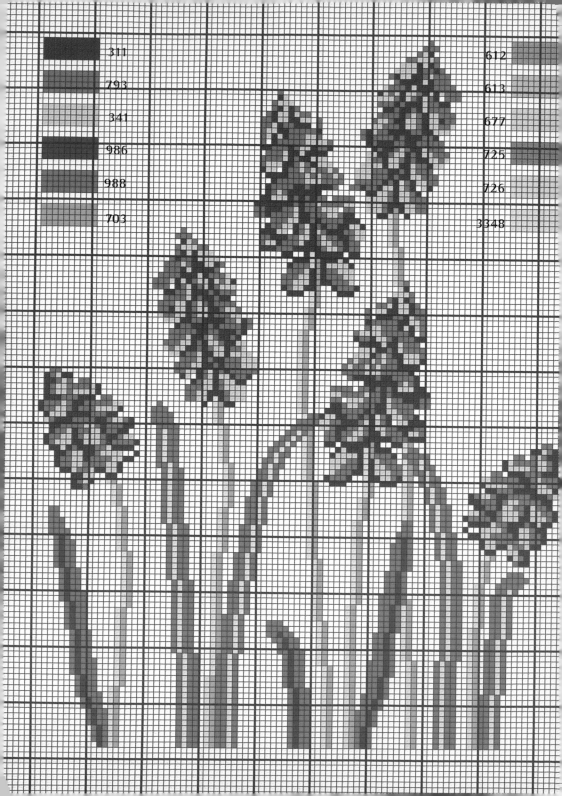

311

793

341

986

988

703

612

613

677

725

726

3348

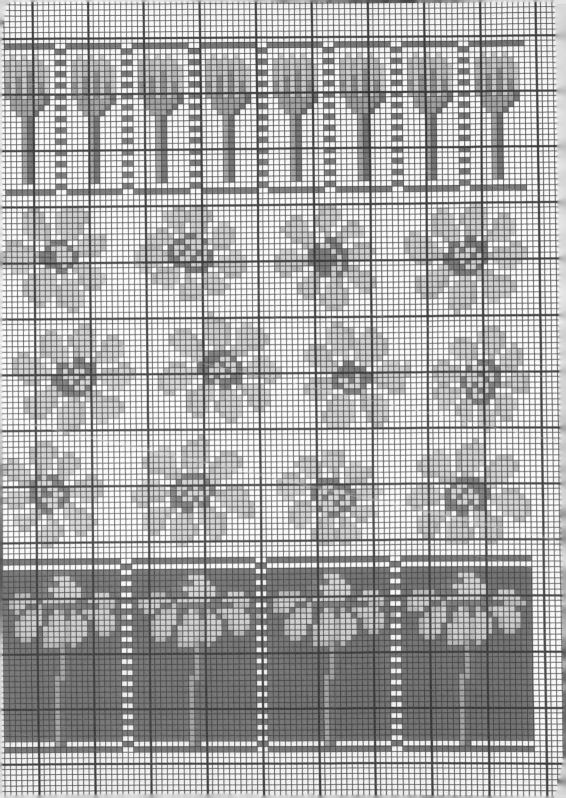

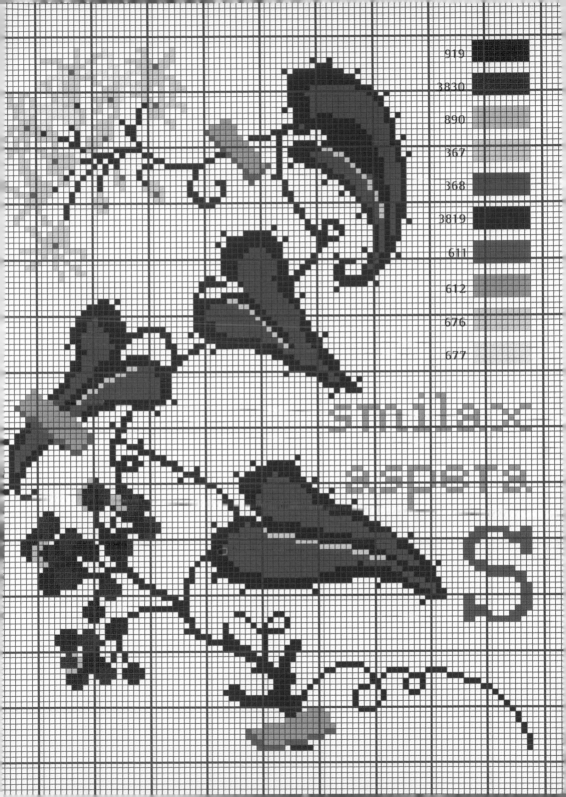

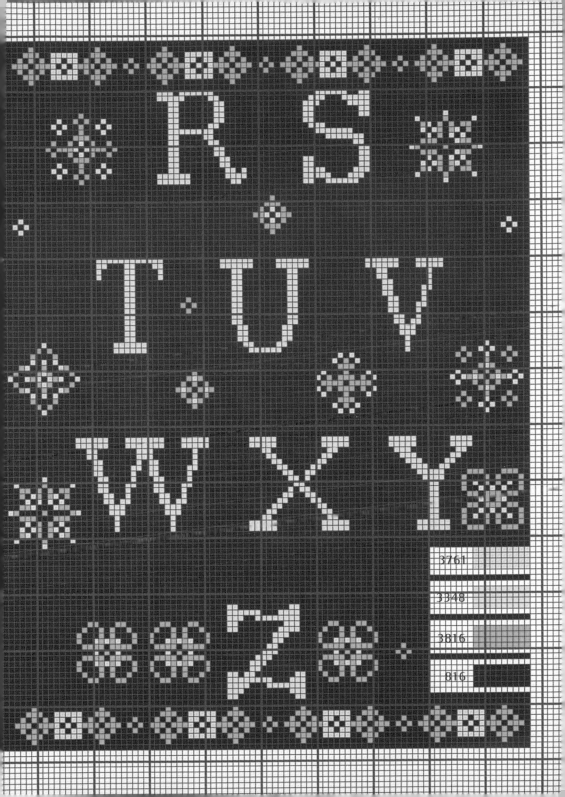

R S

T U V

W X Y

Z

3761

3348

3816

816

3348
988
987
986
341
793
312

3761

518

3765

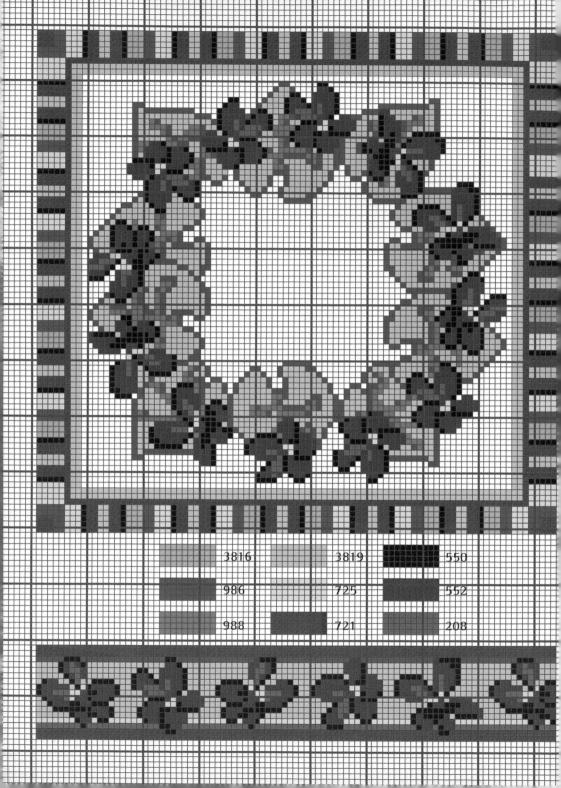

3816   3819   550

986   725   552

988   721   208

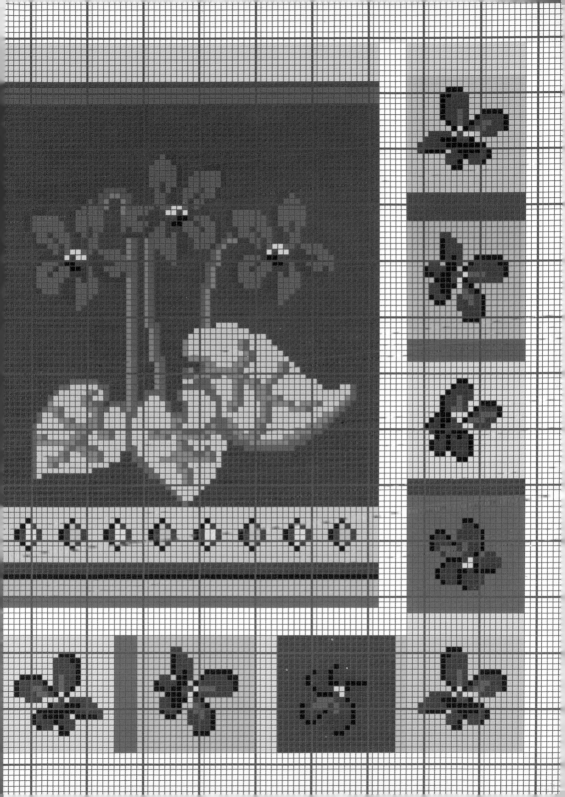

3348, 704, 904, 987 (greens) ; 962, 3706, 3350, 600 (pinks)

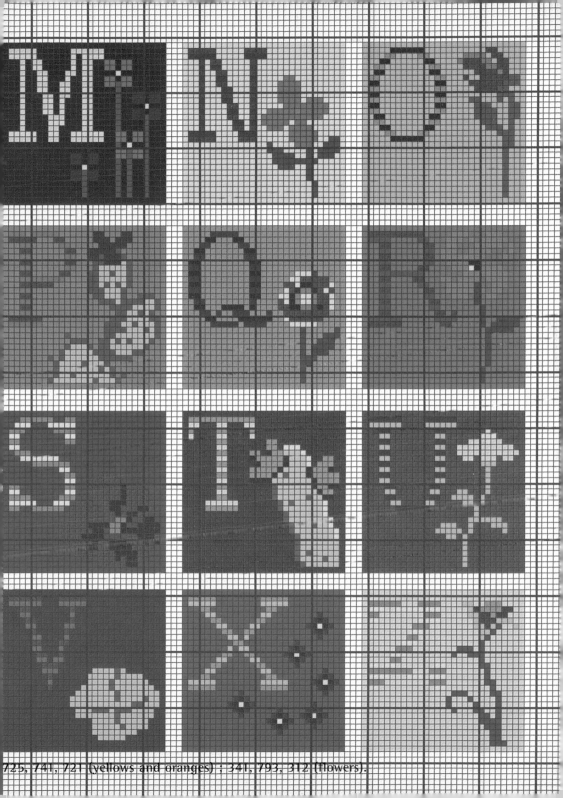

725, 741, 721 (yellows and oranges) ; 341, 793, 312 (flowers).

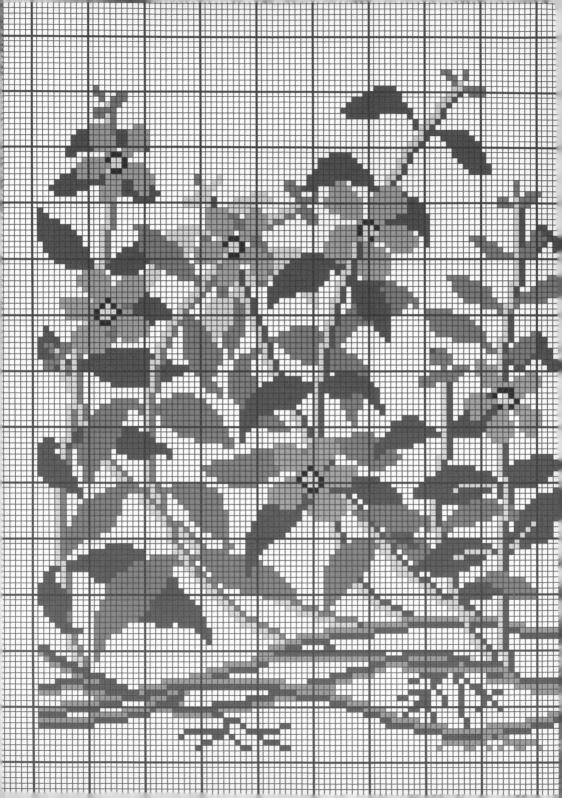

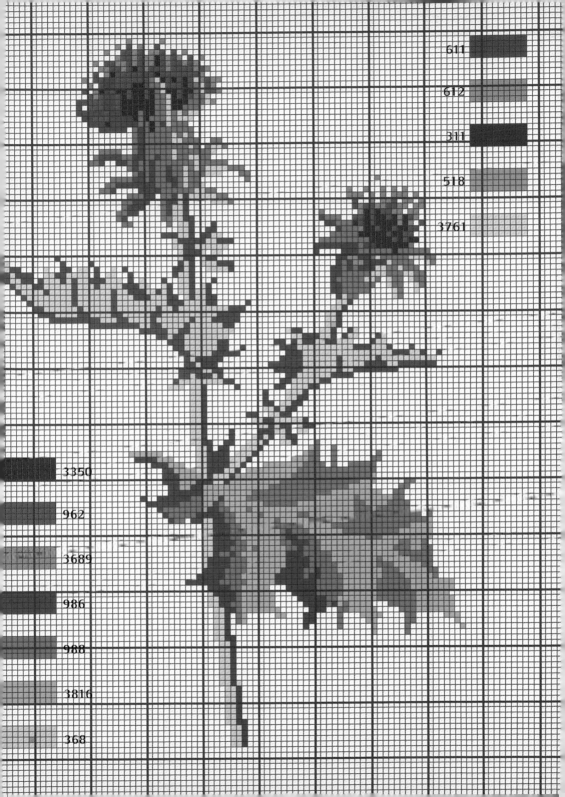

611

612

311

518

3761

3350

962

3689

986

988

3816

368

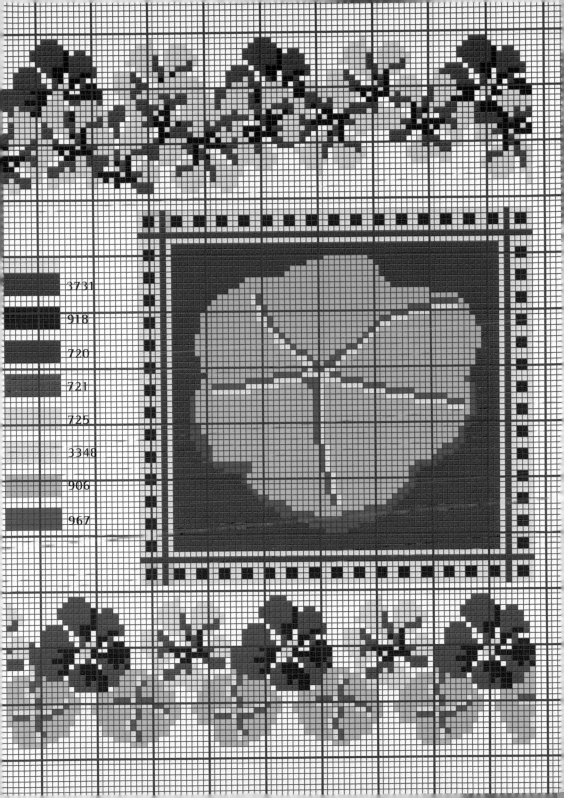

3731

918

720

721

725

3348

906

967

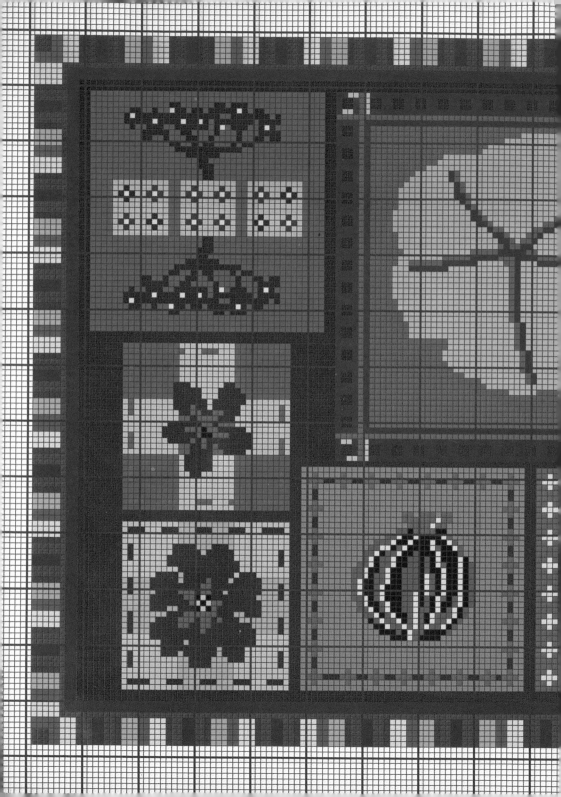

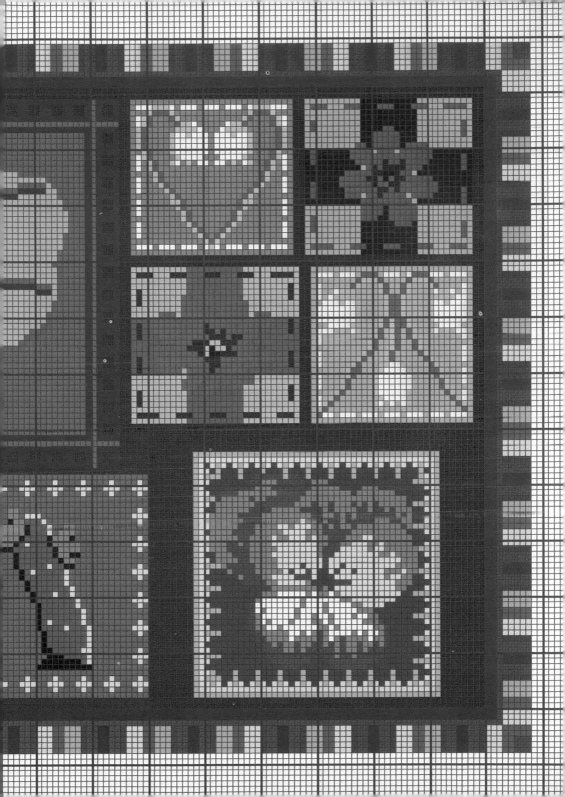

312

793

341

472

906

987

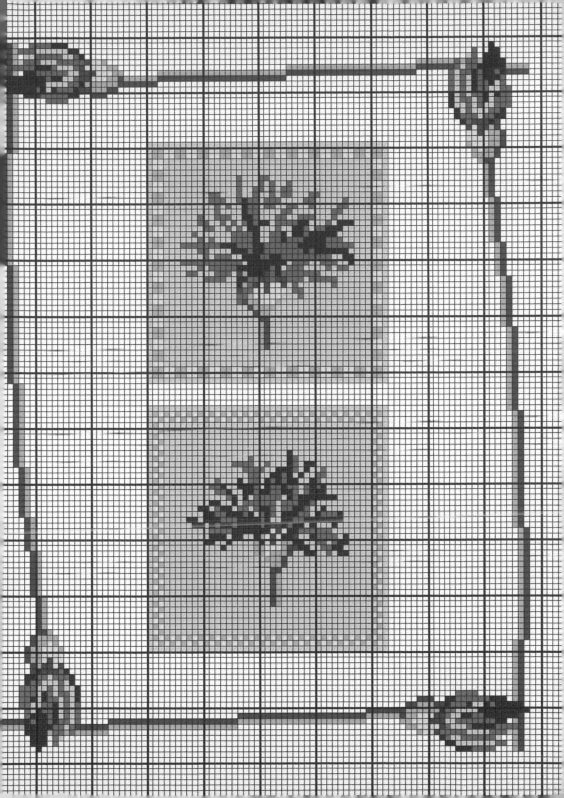

Cross Stitch
Flowers
technical tips

A fun and easy technique

Cross stitch will help you create beautiful pieces of embroidery, and it is deceptively simple to achieve. It is actually one of the easiest stitches – all you need to know is how to count! In the past it was customary for young girls to learn cross stitch, and history has left us with a number of exquisite samplers made by the agile, small hands of these girls. If, like them, you decide to take the plunge, you will see how easily you can achieve remarkable results and how enjoyable cross stitching can be.

The design

Cross stitch embroidery is carried out according to a design on a squared, coloured grid, which forms the pattern. Each square of colour corresponds to a stitch to be embroidered on the fabric. Sometimes the pattern is in black and white and, in this case, different symbols are used for each colour. The same symbol always corresponds to the same colour throughout the piece. Squares with no colour or without a symbol indicate that no stitch is required.

79

If you are a cross stitch beginner, use a fabric known as aida rather than DMC cotton or linen even-weave fabrics. Aida has the advantage of a coarser weft, which closely resembles the squares in the pattern. More experienced stitchers who work on even-weaves will convert each square of the grid on to the fabric by stitching over a group of threads, the number of which will always be identical, both in height and width.

Cross stitch

Cross stitch is elementary both in appearance and in execution. Quite simply, it is made up of two inter-laced diagonal stitches. It can be stitched on its own or continuously. In this case, in order to ensure a beautiful finish, it is important to always stitch the crosses in the same direction, from bottom left to top right; then, on the way back, from bottom right to top left.

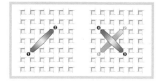

Simple cross stitch

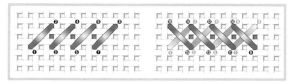

Continuous cross stitch

If you stitch on an even-weave fabric or over one fabric thread, always complete one stitch before moving on to the next. This will ensure that your work is even.

Combining stitches with cross stitch

Some embroidery stitches can be combined with cross stitch to create a look that cross stitch alone cannot achieve, for example to underline a shape.

Important comment

Never make a knot when you start a thread, as it will be seen when the cross stitch is complete and has been ironed. To start a thread length, use your finger to keep hold of a short piece of the thread on the reverse of your work, and work over it with the first stitches to hold it in place.
To end a thread, turn over your work, slip your thread under the last three or four stitches and cut the thread.

You can use half cross stitch, also known as tapestry stitch, to create shadows on the background and soften the colour intensity.

Three-quarter cross stitch allows you to make the edges of a design more precise and is often bordered by a top stitch. This stitch allows you to avoid 'steps' in the sense that the return movement of the thread closes the stitch, either by the right or by the left.

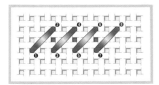

Half cross stitch or tapestry stitch

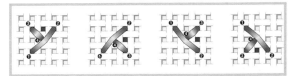

Three-quarter cross stitch

Top stitch is ideal for shaping the design and accentuating it, just as a pencil line would do. It is stitched when the entire cross stitch design is complete. It is done using fewer threads than cross stitch and more often with a colour in a darker tone.

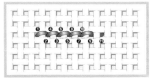

Top stitch

Finally, use a quarter cross stitch to create fine detail. It is used mainly on an even-weave on a single fabric thread.

Tip

If the strands of your thread length become twisted, turn your work over and let your needle hang down loose. The thread will unravel automatically and return to the correct position.

Satin stitch is found on work embroidered on both aida and even-weave fabrics. It creates a smooth, solid area of colour or an outline.

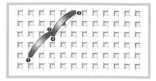

Satin stitch

Preparing the fabric

Before embroidering with cross stitch, you need to prepare the fabric by whipping the edges. This prevents the edges of the fabric from fraying. You could instead apply an adhesive ribbon along the edges of the fabric. The piece of fabric must be a little larger than your embroidery pattern so it can be framed when it is complete.

Fold your fabric into four to find the centre, then tack two rows, one horizontal, the other vertical along the folds. These rows of tacking stitch provide a reference point for stitching and will be removed once the cross stitch is finished. The centre of the design is indicated on the pattern by small arrows located on the sides of the grid. To find the centre of the design, follow the horizontal and vertical axes with your finger, using the arrows.

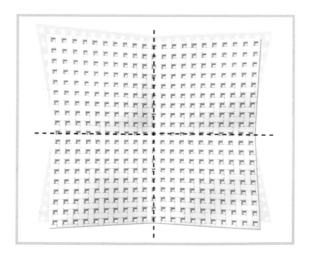

Do not leave long threads at the back of your work. If the stitches in the same colour are approximately 2cm (¾in) apart, you can slip your thread and continue embroidering. If the stitches are further apart (more than 2cm (¾in)), pass the thread under the other stitches, cut, and start again with a new piece of thread.

Finishing

When your cross stitch design is complete, remove the two rows of tacking. Wash the cross stitched fabric gently in cold water and, once dry, iron on the reverse using a damp cloth to protect the fabric.

Framing

Allow at least 7cm (2¾in) around the edges of your work to frame it. Cut a piece of strong cardboard a little smaller than your frame. Place you work on a table, wrong side facing up, and put the cardboard over the top, centring it over the design. Using a strong, thick thread, lace together the upper and lower edges of the work. Be careful not to damage the piece, and tighten the thread regularly to keep the fabric taut. Lace the other two sides together in the same way. Place the laced work in the frame under the glass, and it is finished.

Accessories

Needle

The needle used for cross stitch is a round-ended needle with a wider eye than a sewing needle. Its rounded end does not damage the weft; the size of the eye allows several strands to be threaded through. A No. 26 needle is suitable for working with a single strand, but you will need a No. 24 needle to work with two or three strands. The size of the needle varies according to the weft. Embroidery needles are available to buy in packets of mixed sizes or one size.

Tip

To give relief to your work, you can also place a piece of quilting between the cardboard and the fabric. In this case, your work will not be framed under glass but will be enhanced by the frame you choose. You can also hang your stitched picture using small lengths of wooden beading placed at the top and bottom.

Embroiderers' hoop

Sometimes it is necessary to use a hoop, especially when working on an even-weave or very flexible fabric. It allows you to stretch the fabric and keep the stitches even. Embroiderers' hoops can be fixed on to a table, but we recommend hoops that are easier to carry around with you.

Scissors

Small pointed scissors are best, and use them only for your embroidery. Decorative scissors are available, for example in the shape of a bird, as well as other novelty items for you to hang on the handles so they are easier to find. When you travel, make sure that you keep your scissors separate from your fabric to avoid accidentally cutting your embroidery.

Magnetic board and magnifying rule

Fixing the pattern for your work to a magnetic board allows you to follow the line of your design more easily. The magnifying rule helps you follow the design easily and magnifies it at the same time, which is easier on your eyes.

Boxes for storing threads

You could buy an organiser to keep your threads in. These are cardboard boxes with perforations near the edges which allow you to tidy away your threads and note the reference numbers in the margin.

You could darn your threads on to darning wool boxes and keep each coloured thread in a new box.

Finally, you could use plastic wallets to organise your prepared cardboard sections.

Tip

A needle threader is handy when you need to thread two or three strands together for a single thread length.

Tip

Move the hoop regularly and protect the edges with tissue paper so you don't damage the fabric.

Tip

A thimble will protect your middle finger. If you become a lover of cross stitch you will be forever picking up your work whenever and wherever you can, and you'll be grateful for a thimble!

Tip

Keep a record of the threads you use. This will be useful if you run out of a colour or wish to create the same design again.

Classic fabrics
DMC aida

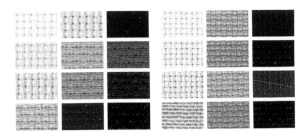

Tip

Before beginning the main design, stitch a test piece to determine the exact number of strands required for the chosen fabric. Too few strands and the thread will not cover the background sufficiently, which could result in a somewhat poor appearance. This would be a shame as the amount of work you have to put in is the same, regardless of the number of strands you use!

Aida is easy to use as the threads form regular squares. It is available in different sizes: 3 stitches, 4 stitches, 5.5 stitches and 7 stitches per centimetre. The size of your work will depend on the fabric you choose. The fewer stitches the fabric has, per centimetre, the larger the finished work will be. For example, embroidery on a 3-stitches per centimetre aida will be much bigger than embroidery on a 7-stitches per centimetre aida.

The table below shows the approximate length of the fabric, in centimetres, for ten stitches. If you already have an idea of the size of your project, these conversion references might be useful.

Aida fabric	Length for ten stitches	Number of strands to use
3 stitches/cm	3.1cm (1¼in)	Three or four
4 stitches/cm	2.5cm (1in)	Three
5.5 stitches/cm	1.81cm (¾in)	Two or three
7 stitches/cm	1.4cm (½in)	One or two

DMC even-weave and linen fabric

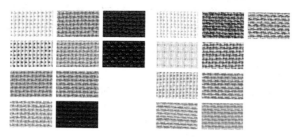

Using linen or cotton allows you to choose the size of your cross stitches. They are a little more difficult to use than aida as they are not woven in squares but this difficulty is largely offset by a more refined result.

Stitching over two

The table below shows the expected sizes if you stitch each cross over two fabric threads in height and width.

Linen fabrics	Length for ten stitches	Number of strands to use
8 count [8 threads/cm]	2.5cm (1in)	Three or four
10 count	2cm (¾in)	Two or three
11 count	1.82cm (½in)	Two or three
12 count	1.66cm (½in)	One or two
14 count	1.4cm (½in)	One

Even-weave	Length for ten stitches	Number of strands to use
10 threads/cm	2cm (¾in)	Two or three

Tip

All these fabrics exist in numerous colours, either by the metre or as remnants. Do not hesitate to ask your haberdasher for advice.

Stitching over one

The table below shows the expected sizes if you stitch each cross over one fabric thread in height and width.

Tip

If you are stitching on dark fabric, place a pale cloth over your knees to help you see more easily where to insert your needle.

Linen fabrics	Length for ten stitches	Number of strands to use
8 count	1.25cm (½in)	One
10 count	1cm (½in)	One
11 count	0.9cm (½in)	One
12 count	0.83cm (½in)	One

Cotton even-weave	Length for ten stitches	Number of strands to use
10 count	1cm (½in)	One

Pre-cut fabrics

DMC aida, linen fabric or even-weave are available in a variety of colours, either by the metre or as remnants. These pre-cut fabrics are available in two sizes: 35 × 47cm (14 × 18½in) and 50 × 78cm (19½ × 30½in).

Tip

To find out the number of threads per centimetre of a fabric you want to turn into a tablecloth for example, place two pins 1cm (½in) apart and count the threads between them

Dream fabrics

Do you want to embroider a tablecloth, a bath towel or a bib? Do you want to decorate a pretty tea towel with designs? There are numerous products available to allow you to do so, and you will find many kits in shops to satisfy your growing passion.

Let's imagine that your fabric is 10 count and your design is 52 stitches over 52. If you work over two fabric threads, this is 10÷2 = 5 stitches/cm, and your work will therefore be 52÷5 = 10.4cm (4in). If you work over three fabric threads, this is 10÷3 = 3.33 stitches/cm, and your work will be 52÷3.33 = 15.62cm (6in).

These values are approximate as they depend on how tightly you stitch.

Vinyl or carded fabrics

These are often used for small embroidered items, such as bookmarks or to make mobiles or birthday cake decorations. Stitch the chosen design and cut out, either around the edge of the design or in the shape of the finished item (for example, an extended rectangle for a bookmark).

Pulled-thread fabric

This even-weave fabric is designed specifically for pulled thread work and allows you to stitch on any background fabric. Use a hoop to hold the work in place, then stitch the design using the pulled-thread fabric fixed to the surface of your chosen background fabric.

Pulled-thread fabric

Cross stitches are made through the two thicknesses of fabric. When the design is complete, pull the threads of the pulled-thread fabric one by one using tweezers. The cross stitches will remain on the background fabric.

Canvas

Canvas is a fairly stiff fabric and is available in several weights. It is usually made of cotton or linen and varies in the tightness of the weave. It is ideal for making cushions and chair or sofa covers, but you can also use it as a pulled-thread fabric. Simply dampen your work and, using tweezers, pull the threads of the canvas one by one.

Threads

DMC Mouliné stranded cotton

Mouliné stranded cotton thread has a shiny appearance and is available in about 460 colours. Mouliné stranded cotton is the thread most often used for cross stitch. It has six strands that are easily separated. Available in variegated shades, these produce a wonderful effect in your finished embroidery but demand no more effort from the stitcher than a plain stranded cotton thread.

Tip

If you work with variegated Mouliné stranded cotton, complete one stitch at a time before moving on to the next so there isn't too much of a difference in tone between the thread lengths. When you begin a new thread length, take care to start with the same tone. If you finish with a light tone, start again with a light tone and similarly with a dark tone.

DMC metallic Mouliné stranded cotton

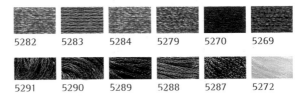

| 5282 | 5283 | 5284 | 5279 | 5270 | 5269 |

| 5291 | 5290 | 5289 | 5288 | 5287 | 5272 |

This thread is presented in two ways: in the form of either a six-strand skein or a three-strand bobbin. Sixteen colours are available, including bicoloured and multicoloured threads.

You can also mix a strand of metallic Mouliné stranded cotton with a strand of traditional Mouliné stranded cotton in very close colours to produce a different effect. Experiment by replacing traditional Mouliné stranded cotton with metallic Mouliné stranded cotton. Your work will take on a completely different appearance!

Tip

Metallic thread can split easily as you work, so use a sewing needle with a small eye and only use small lengths.

The table below will help you find the traditional Mouliné stranded cotton and the corresponding metallic Mouliné stranded cotton.

Metallics	5272	5289	5288	5291	5290	5287
Traditional Mouliné stranded cotton	5200	209	316	798	806	413
Metallics	5282	5283	5284	5279	5270	5269
Traditional Mouliné stranded cotton	834	762	833	3064	816	3818

DMC matt-folded thread

This non-divisible thread is suitable for use with thick cotton fabrics.

Pearl cotton No. 3, No. 5 and No. 8

Pearl cotton is available in skeins or balls and has a satin appearance. There are 292 shades of pearl cotton No. 3, 312 shades of No. 5 and 238 shades of No. 8.

This shiny looking thread, which considerably enhances stitching work, is used on thick fabrics, for example to embroider tablecloths, place mats and other table linen.

Multicoloured pearl cotton

Multicoloured pearl cotton, also known as Castelbajac thread, varies gradually from one colour to the next along its length. It should be stitched using the same technique as the variegated Mouliné stranded cotton, on a thick fabric, as this thread is a pearl cotton No. 8.

Medicis wool

You can also use wool for your cross stitch work. When used on linen, Medicis wool gives an antique appearance. It is available in 178 colours.

Creative ideas

Tip for adventurous stitchers

You can add more depth and style to your work by mixing the threads. Mixing threads is fun, and creates unique and sometimes surprising results. To add subtle shading, mix a strand of light coloured Mouliné stranded cotton with a strand of darker Mouliné stranded cotton in the same tonal range.

Experiment with the number of thread strands according to your fabric; the more strands you stitch with, the denser the colour. You can create more delicate and light embroidery using fewer strands.

If you have a design of your own that you'd like to embroider in cross stitch, you first need to convert it into a cross stitch pattern using transparent, squared paper. You can find this in haberdashery shops, and it is specially designed for this purpose.

It is best to choose a simple design as too much detail can ruin the work. Place the squared paper over the design and trace the outline with a pencil. To make a cross stitch pattern, change the shapes by adapting each line to a series of squares.

When drawing your pattern, if your pencil line is in the centre or in the upper part of a square, colour the square above; but colour the square below if the pencil line is in the lower part of the square. Colour the squares on your pattern with coloured pencils to match the design you are copying. You are now ready to stitch your own creation!

DMC Mouliné stranded cotton

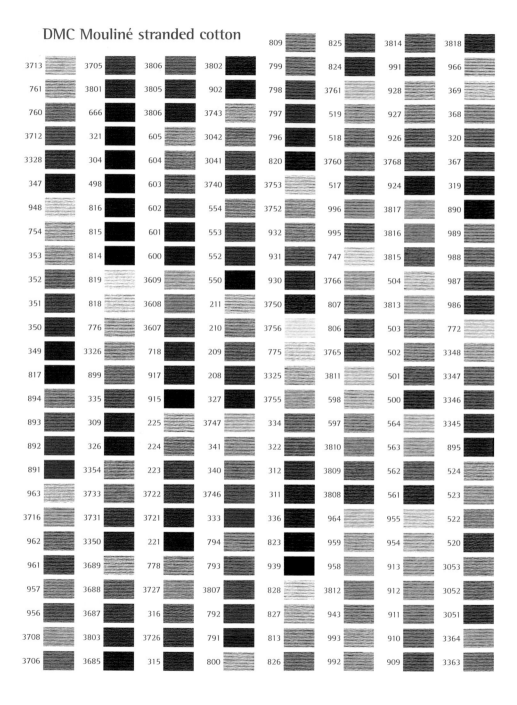

				809	825	3814	3818	
3713	3705	3806	3802	799	824	991	966	
761	3801	3805	902	798	3761	928	369	
760	666	3806	3743	797	519	927	368	
3712	321	605	3042	796	518	926	320	
3328	304	604	3041	820	3760	3768	367	
347	498	603	3740	3753	517	924	319	
948	816	602	554	3752	996	3817	890	
754	815	601	553	932	995	3816	989	
353	814	600	552	931	747	3815	988	
352	819	3609	550	930	3766	504	987	
351	818	3608	211	3750	807	3813	986	
350	776	3607	210	3756	806	503	772	
349	3326	718	209	775	3765	502	3348	
817	899	917	208	3325	3811	501	3347	
894	335	915	327	3755	598	500	3346	
893	309	225	3747	334	597	564	3345	
892	326	224	341	322	3810	563	895	
891	3354	223	340	312	3809	562	524	
963	3733	3722	3746	311	3808	561	523	
3716	3731	3721	333	336	964	955	522	
962	3350	221	794	823	959	954	520	
961	3689	778	793	939	958	913	3053	
957	3688	3727	3807	828	3812	912	3052	
956	3687	316	792	827	943	911	3051	
3708	3803	3726	791	813	993	910	3364	
3706	3685	315	800	826	992	909	3363	

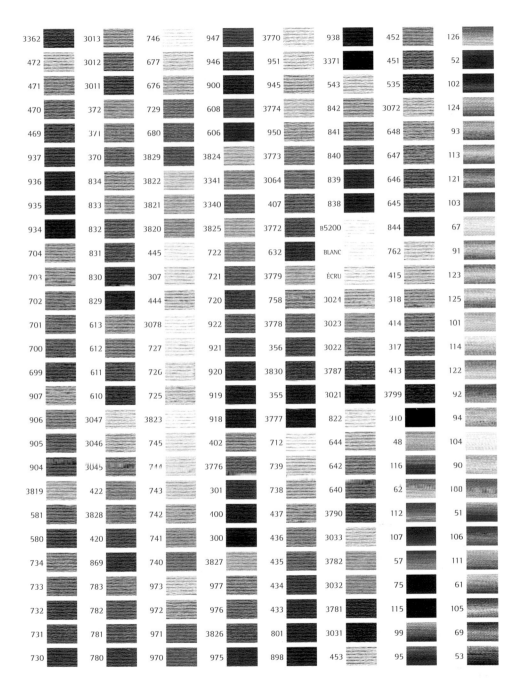

3362	3013	746	947	3770	938	452	126
472	3012	677	946	951	3371	451	52
471	3011	676	900	945	543	535	102
470	372	729	608	3774	842	3072	124
469	371	680	606	950	841	648	93
937	370	3829	3824	3773	840	647	113
936	834	3822	3341	3064	839	646	121
935	833	3821	3340	407	838	645	103
934	832	3820	3825	3772	B5200	844	67
704	831	445	722	632	BLANC	762	91
703	830	307	721	3779	ÉCRU	415	123
702	829	444	720	758	3024	318	125
701	613	3078	922	3778	3023	414	101
700	612	727	921	356	3022	317	114
699	611	726	920	3830	3787	413	122
907	610	725	919	355	3021	3799	92
906	3047	3823	918	3777	822	310	94
905	3046	745	402	712	644	48	104
904	3045	744	3776	739	642	116	90
3819	422	743	301	738	640	62	100
581	3828	742	400	437	3790	112	51
580	420	741	300	436	3033	107	106
734	869	740	3827	435	3782	57	111
733	783	973	977	434	3032	75	61
732	782	972	976	433	3781	115	105
731	781	971	3826	801	3031	99	69
730	780	970	975	898	453	95	53

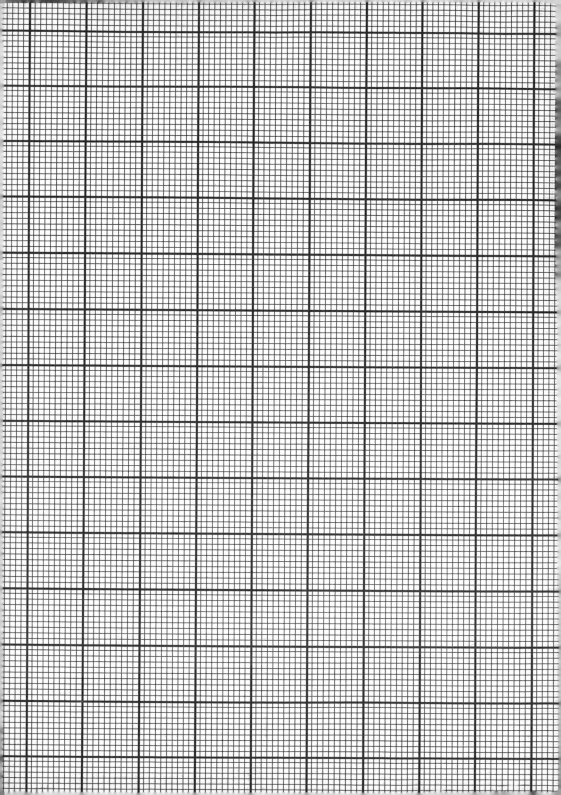

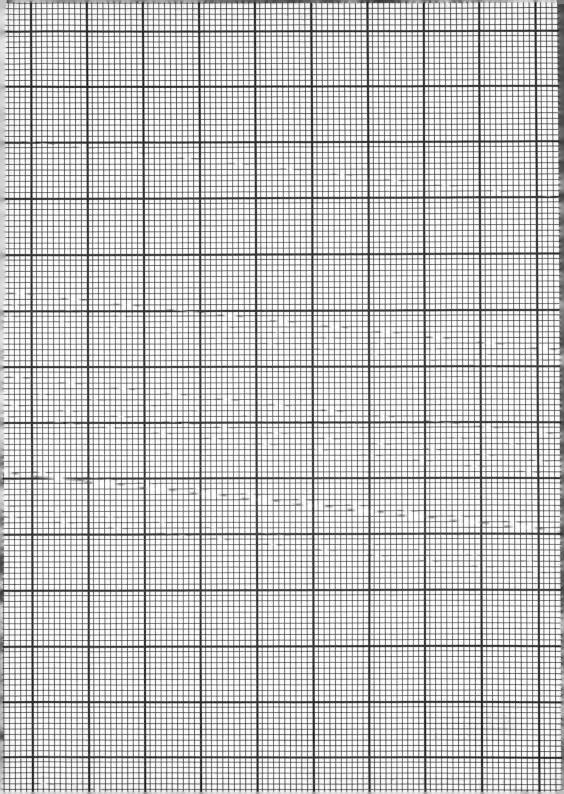

We would like to thank Potiron,
for its kind cooperation with this work,
as well as Nathalie Renault, Vanessa Nonnereau
and Francine Ledent for creating the embroidery
designs and, finally, Véronique Violette and
Isabelle Contreau for their tips and
encouragement.